Published By Robert Corbin

@ Toby Desir

Grow Rich: Key Ideas From Think and Grow Rich

Original Book

All Right RESERVED

ISBN 978-87-94477-82-6

TABLE OF CONTENTS

Chapter 1 1

The Most Powerful Thoughts: Guided By Your Heart 1

Chapter 2 19

The Power Of Your Mind 19

Chapter 3 27

Comprehend Where You're At 27

Chapter 4 36

Overcoming Limiting Beliefs 36

Chapter 5 43

Money Mindset 43

Chapter 6 49

A Summary Of Forgiveness, Awareness, And Unity 49

Chapter 7 72

The Starting Point Of All Achievement............................ 72

Chapter 8 77

The Principle Of Power 77

When You Become Quiet, It Just Dawns On You 77

Chapter 9 99

Principles Of Think And Grow Rich: How To Use Your Mind To Create Wealth 99

Chapter 1

The Most Powerful Thoughts: Guided by Your Heart

As I begin writing this chapter, I find myself contemplating the voyage I have undertaken in the past few years. It has been a rollercoaster ride, full of twists and turns, plot twists, highs and lows, and everything in between. In fact, this book only took me two weeks to write from start to finish because I chose to listen to my heart and not sit on the information it was giving me. The most powerful thoughts are the ones guided by your heart. You see when the heart calls you must go. Do not wait because if you do not do what the heart is guiding you to do it may be too late. I have learned that the most powerful thoughts are simply reminding the mind of what the heart already knows. For me, feeling my heart again was a process well worth it.

First, I had to find out that I was walking around like a zombie pretending that everything was ok and living my life through my mind's eye and thought that because I had all the fancy stuff and material wealth this made me happy. It was only some twisted idea of real happiness not having anything to do with the heart but rather an accumulation of resources disguised as happiness and fulfillment. Through some of the practices I will share in this book, I regained the connection with my heart's GPS; I just needed a reboot and for me that was death. Your reboot does not have to be death it can be this book or perhaps a conversation with a friend or a flash of insight while cooking dinner. In whatever way, your reboot shows up, be on alert, pay attention, and follow your heart's guidance.

It took time, patience, and a lot of self-reflection. But as I started to reconnect with my heart, I realized that it was the key to unlocking my true potential and living a life of purpose and meaning. I had lost my way in the murky waters we sometimes call life. I had lost my sense of self, believing that if I only loved someone enough, they would love me back, or if I cared enough and provided enough then my family and friends would love me. But that never worked out for me because the premise was that I had to actually do something to feel something and that is not how it works.

You do not have to do anything or be anybody to know you are loved and you are LOVE. Your DNA is love and you are infinitely loved across all time, space, and dimensions. That is the truth. This is the premise of our true wealth and being rich is all about this. In fact, "The God Code" by Gregg Braden is a book that explores the relationship between science and spirituality it suggests that the DNA in our cells holds a code that represents a message from God. Braden argues that the ancient Hebrew alphabet holds the key to unlocking this code, and that by understanding the language and meaning behind the letters, we can uncover a deeper understanding of the universe and our place in it. Braden's research on the DNA signature of God suggests that the sequence of letters in the Hebrew alphabet corresponds to the sequence of nucleotides in our DNA. He argues that this is evidence that our DNA is not random, but rather has been designed with a purpose by a higher intelligence. Braden's theory on this is fascinating and it is worth exploring. (Braden, 2023)

So, what are the most powerful thoughts we can have to help us feel our hearts again? Here are a few that have worked for me. These are not affirmation or self-help incantations but rather a series of thoughts that are available not for you to believe them but for you to simply remind your mind via your heart's intelligence that you are in fact these emotions. You see the heart is like a motor and its fuel is emotions. The way you get your heart's attention is by intention and tapping lightly in the area of the heart and by simply expressing these emotions your heart will remind your mind that it is in fact so.

It is easy to get lost in our own thoughts and allow our fears to control us. We often forget that deep down, our hearts already know what we need to feel whole and fulfilled. It is important to remind our minds of this truth, and we can do that by incorporating powerful thoughts into our daily lives. Always remember that it is never the thoughts first but the emotion that the heart feels then the thoughts come, and then magic happens. The sequence is important because science has proven that the heart sends more signals to the brain than the brain to the heart and therefore, we can presume that the heart is the master controller.

Remind your mind what the heart already knows:

I choose love over fear.

By choosing to love over fear, we allow ourselves to act from a place of compassion and empathy. This reminds us to connect with others and approach life with an open heart.

I am deserving of my own forgiveness.

Forgiving ourselves is crucial to letting go of past mistakes and moving forward. We must remember that we are human and deserving of self-compassion.

I let go of what no longer serves me.

Letting go of what no longer serves us allows us to make space for new experiences and opportunities. It reminds us to prioritize our well-being and only hold onto what brings us joy and fulfillment.

I trust that everything happens for my highest good.

Trusting that everything happens for our highest good allows us to let go of our need for control and surrender to the journey of life. It reminds us that every experience has a purpose and a lesson to teach us.

I am enough just as I am.

Reminding ourselves that we are enough just as we are essential to self-love and acceptance. It reminds us to embrace our unique qualities and appreciate ourselves for who we are.

I am grateful for the lesson's life has taught me.

Being grateful for the lesson's life has taught us allows us to shift our perspective and focus on the positive. It reminds us to appreciate every experience, whether good or bad, as an opportunity for growth.

I embrace change and welcome new opportunities.

Embracing change and welcoming new opportunities allows us to step outside our comfort zone and grow. It reminds us to be open to new experiences and to approach life with curiosity and excitement.

I am in control of my thoughts and emotions.

Taking control of our thoughts and emotions is crucial to our mental and emotional well-being. It reminds us that we have the power to shape our own reality.

I release the need to control everything around me.

Releasing the need to control everything around us allows us to let go of our fears and anxieties. It reminds us to trust the universe and surrender to the flow of life.

I am open to receiving love and abundance.

Being open to receiving love and abundance reminds us to approach life with a positive attitude and an open heart. It reminds us that we are deserving of all the good things life has to offer.

I am worthy of all the good things life has to offer.

Reminding ourselves that we are worthy of all the good things life has to offer is essential to self-love and acceptance. It reminds us to prioritize our own well-being and to embrace our unique qualities.

I am at peace with myself and my surroundings.

Being at peace with ourselves and our surroundings allows us to approach life with a sense of calm and serenity. It reminds us to appreciate the beauty around us and to focus on the present moment.

I honor my body and treat it with love and respect.

Honoring our bodies and treating them with love and respect is crucial to our physical and mental well-being. It reminds us to prioritize self-care and to appreciate the vessel that carries us through life.

I choose kindness and compassion in all my interactions.

Choosing kindness and compassion in all our interactions reminds us to approach life with empathy and understanding. It reminds us to connect with others and to be a positive force in the world.

I am surrounded by positivity and good energy.

Surrounding ourselves with positivity and good energy reminds us to focus on the good in life and to approach challenges with a positive attitude.

I am constantly growing and evolving.

Reminding ourselves that we are constantly growing and evolving at our own pace and that life is not a race or a competition but rather an experience that is so unique that it is once in a lifetime.

When we live our life from a place of fear, we limit ourselves and hold ourselves back from experiencing all the wonderful things life has to offer. Fear causes us to play small, avoid risks and challenges, and settle for less than we deserve. It keeps us stuck in a place of scarcity and negativity, preventing us from seeing the beauty and abundance around us. On the other hand, choosing to love over fear opens us up to a world of possibilities.

When we operate from a place of love, we see ourselves and others in a positive light. We take risks, pursue our passions, and live life to the fullest. We recognize that we are deserving of all the good things life has to offer and we go after them with confidence and courage.

Forgiveness

is also an important part of feeling our hearts again. When we forgive ourselves, we release the negative emotions and self-judgment that hold us back from fully embracing our true selves. We recognize that we are only human and that we deserve our own forgiveness. This helps us let go of the past and move forward in a more positive and productive way.

Letting go

of what no longer serves us is another powerful thought that can help us feel our hearts again. We all have things in our lives that no longer serve us, whether it be relationships, jobs, habits, or beliefs. When we let go of these things, we create space for new opportunities and experiences that align with our true selves.

Trusting

that everything happens for our highest good is also an important thought to have. When we trust in the universe and believe that everything happens for a reason, we become more open to new experiences and opportunities. We learn to let go of the need to control everything around us and to embrace change as a natural part of life.

Believing that we are enough just as we are, is crucial to feeling our hearts again. We live in a society that often tells us we are not enough, and that we need to do more or be more to be happy and successful. When we believe that we are enough just as we are, we stop seeking external validation and start living from a place of self-acceptance and self-love.

Appreciation is another powerful thought that can help us feel our hearts again. When we focus on all the things, we have to be grateful for, we shift our perspective and start to see the world in a more positive light. We become more present and mindful in our daily lives, and we appreciate the little things that bring us joy and happiness. In the book "Thank and Grow Rich" by Pam Grout she encourages readers to cultivate an attitude of gratitude in their daily lives in order to manifest more abundance, joy, and fulfillment. The book is inspired by the principles of Napoleon Hill's classic self-help book, "Think and Grow Rich," but with a focus on the power of gratitude. Now, I love this book and think everyone should read it and I also was inspired by Napoleon Hill's classic book however I found that not enough emphasis was placed on the power of the heart and the research behind it, so this is why I wrote this book to complement Grout's wonderful work along with Hill's work.

Embracing change and welcoming new opportunities is also important to feel our hearts again. Change can be scary and uncomfortable, but it is also a necessary part of growth and evolution. When we embrace change and welcome new opportunities, we open ourselves up to new experiences and possibilities that can bring us closer to our true selves.

Ultimately, reminding our minds of what our hearts already know is crucial to living a fulfilling and authentic life. When we choose love over fear, forgive ourselves, let go of what no longer serves us, trust in the universe, believe in our own worth, and cultivate appreciation and openness, we create space for joy, abundance, and fulfillment in our lives. We become more connected to our true selves and to the world around us, and we start living from a place of authenticity, purpose, and love.

The most powerful thoughts to help you feel your heart again are those that are backed by your emotions. When I first learned this and understood that it was my emotions that fueled my heart, I knew that now I had the key to feeling my heart again and also gaining momentum on my manifestation powers. It's fascinating to understand the heart in this way but as you will see in the chapters to come this way of thinking about the heart and body dates back thousands of years.

My hope is that I can help you in understanding these basic heart principles and how our most treasured wisdom keepers have used the heart's power to feel the world in a different way and to manifest their heart's desires. Never doubt that the most powerful thoughts you have that are linked to joy, happiness and abundance are guided by your heart.

Chapter 2

The Power of Your Mind

We live in an increasingly competitive world that often demands the best of us. Growing rich can be a difficult and challenging transition, and reaching financial freedom is often deemed to be an impossible dream by those who attempt it. However, the truth is that nearly anyone can become financially successful if they have the will to do it. With the right mindset, anyone can use the power of their mind to plan, execute, and grow their wealth.

The mind is an incredibly powerful tool that has been given to us to succeed in life. It is essential to understand how our minds are capable of growth and how it can be used to reach our goals. Most importantly, it can be utilized to create a positive and productive thought pattern. The power of the mind, combined with diligent planning and guidance, is an approachable goal in terms of becoming financially successful. It is possible to become financially rich and successful if one knows where to begin.

This book will explore the power of the mind and how one can use it to grow their wealth. We will discuss some of the mental techniques to help you think proactively and set yourself up for success. We will also provide various strategies for wise financial spending, investment strategies, and tips for becoming wealthy.

The Power of the Mind for Financial Success

The power of the mind is an incredibly powerful tool in achieving any goal, especially financial success. By utilizing the power of the mind, one can gain clarity and focus in life. Thinking positively and engaging in creative problem-solving can help you focus on managing your finances more effectively.

The power of the mind can also help you to focus on planning and setting realistic benchmarks for success. By taking the time to plan, it can be easier to determine the best route to financial success. Having a plan for becoming debt free, increasing savings, and investing is essential when working towards financial success.

In addition to planning, the power of the mind can help you to commit to freeing up time to focus on financial and investment goals. Learning about wiser spending and investing, as well as developing a budget, is essential. When you use the power of the mind to focus on the task at hand, it can make a huge difference in how quickly you reach your goals.

Wise Financial Spending and Investment Strategies

When it comes to growing wealth, it is important to practice wise spending and strategically investing. Wise spending means only purchasing things that you need and avoiding wasting money on items that will not serve you in the future. It also means investing in yourself and your future by putting money into retirement accounts as well as other investments.

When it comes to investing, it is important to do research and take the time to strategize. Investing requires a certain level of risk-tolerance and it is essential to know your own boundaries. It might be beneficial to find an expert in the field or an experienced financial planner to guide you in the right direction.

Another essential component in growing your wealth is to diversify your portfolio. This means investing in multiple areas and stocks such as domestic and international markets, real estate, and independent businesses. Diversifying your investments can help you to take fewer risks and balance out your portfolio, which can be essential when it comes to growing your wealth.

Tips for Becoming Financially Rich

Becoming financially rich is a goal that many have, and it is an attainable one when you are willing to work hard and make sacrifices. Here are some tips for achieving financial success:

1. Set realistic goals: It is important to have a growth plan and clear goals so that you know

where you are aiming for and what measurable actions you need to take.

2. Keep track of your finances: Staying informed about your current finances is the best way to create a smart financial plan. Track your income and spending as well as other financial commitments like debt and investments.

3. Invest for growth: Investing in stocks and other assets is essential for growing your money over time. Investing in mutual funds or foreign markets can help you diversify your portfolio and minimize your financial risk.

4. Automate your savings: Automation can help you save more money without you having to think about it. Consider setting up savings goals and automatic transfers to help you reach them.

5. Be smart with debt: If you are in debt, it is important to prioritize paying it off. Consider setting up a plan to help you become debt free as soon as possible.

Chapter 3

Comprehend Where You're At

You can't accomplish independence from the rat race without knowing your beginning stage. Taking a gander at the amount of obligation you possess, how much investment funds you don't have, and how much cash you want can be a discouraging reality. However, this is an important positive development.

Incorporate a rundown of every one of your obligations: contract, understudy loans, vehicle advance, Visas, and some other obligation you might have gathered. Remember to incorporate any cash you might have acquired from companions or relatives throughout the long term.

Presently, take a full breath. What's more, another. Then, at that point, include every one of the numbers.

How much obligation do you have?

Assuming that it's a major number, don't go crazy, I guarantee I'll share far to pay that down later in this article. In the event that it's a modest number, congrats! Go ahead and share your independence from the rat race tips in the remarks beneath.

Then, investigate all the cash you have set aside.

Incorporate a rundown of every one of your reserve funds: investment accounts, stocks, organization stock-matching projects, organization retirement-matching projects, and retirement plans. Then, at that point, we'll add the repetitive regularly scheduled installments you get like compensation, side gig cash, etc.

Remember these numbers as we work through the following couple of independence from the rat race tips.

The initial step to independence from the rat race is to ensure you grasp your monetary scene.

So what precisely does monetary scene mean? In the broadest feeling of the term, monetary scene depicts all your cash coming in and all your cash going out.

You can consider your monetary scene being made out of the accompanying:

    resources

    open doors

plans

applications

Resources (any asset that you own that ought to give a future advantage) alone don't make up a monetary scene — we are excessively near our undeniable resources for see genuine potential. For the time being, pause for a minute to investigate and ponder whether you have any of the accompanying significant things in your monetary scene:

Do you possess a house or some other genuine property?

Do you have a vehicle, boat, or sporting vehicle that is seldom utilized?

Do you have a legacy or maybe one looking for you from a trust or will?

Do you have extra security with a money esteem or an annuity?

Do you or your life partner at present have an IRA?

Do you have cash in a current or changed over boss' retirement plan

Do you have a benefits from a division or association?

Do you know the most perfect chance to get to your federal retirement aide?

Do you routinely have a duty discount? How could you at any point manage this discount?

Is it true that you are presently getting any extra pay like divorce settlement, side business, or federal retirement aide while you are north of 65 yet working?

Do you have some work right now, or would you say you will work?

Is your spending focused on? Has it been explored and assessed?

What Are Your Spending Patterns?

It is basic to comprehend your spending designs since there is frequently "covered up spending" that we neglect or limit its effect. Gift giving and cleaning are two of those secret costs. Frequently you rebate their channel on pay and don't perceive that the couple of hundred spent every month on these "necessities" are decreasing your capacity to take care of obligation or expand your investment funds.

Your Saving Opportunities

It is vital to understand that while you are in your procuring years, when your service association or business offers a retirement bundle or plan, pick in right away. Anyway little you contribute, it will be decisively significant for yourself as well as your family with regards to "living" and partaking in your retirement of importance and reason.

Obligations, Liabilities, Skills, and Capabilities Your monetary scene additionally incorporates your obligations and liabilities in addition to your abilities and capacities. Your liabilities — what you owe — is significant on the grounds that it confines your decisions and limits your choices. Your liabilities make a boundary to pushing ahead and kicking off your Future Funded Ministry.

Liabilities make a mental blockade holding you back from understanding your Future Funded Ministry and what it ought to resemble. Then again, your abilities, and experiential learning capacities structure a significant starting point for your monetary scene. This is your ability to make worth and hence to create economical resources and usable assets. Essentially expressed, you will have more cash.

Simple Keys to a Sound Financial Landscape

Here are a few significant hints to assist you with setting up your monetary scene:

Live on what you make.

Set up an arrangement for escaping obligation. Comprehend how you and your life partner view cash and settle on monetary choices. This is basic to both your preparation and execution of the arrangement.

Make a retirement plan and pick the speculation vehicles that are generally material to your gamble profile, age, remaining chance to retirement, cash character, and reserve funds approach. Your Financial Landscape Defined

More or less, the resources you have, in addition to your on-going profit, short your ongoing obligation level, alongside the methodology and plans that you and your life partner are making together form your monetary scene.

Every one of us has a monetary scene. This is the ideal opportunity for you to recognize what it is, foster elective activity plans, and assume responsibility for your future.

Chapter 4

Overcoming Limiting Beliefs

- Increasing my wealth just depends on me choosing to.
- I can come up with wonderful ideas to increase my wealth.
- There is always an opportunity to make more money.
- I can make real what I see in my mind.
- I can create the life I deserve and want with the skills that I currently have.
- I can create the life I deserve and want with the means that I currently have.
- The only thing that could ever hold me back is myself.
- Every difficulty is possible to overcome.
- Nobody else controls my success but me.

- I find it easy to make more money.
- I can create anything and make it grow as large as I want.
- The amount of money in the world is unlimited—I just have to attract it to me.
- I find it easy to create new businesses and seize new opportunities.
- I see joy, happiness, and abundance everywhere I go.
- I accept the riches and money that freely and constantly come into my life.
- Wealth often comes to me in unexpected ways.
- My fortune is already there, it is just waiting for me to go get it.
- The universe is glorious and full of infinite love.
- I am a naturally happy and successful person who is destined for a wonderful life.

- I am capable of generating wealth just as much as anyone else.
- I deserve to be rich just as much as anyone else.
- Wealth is attracted to me and I can access it at any time.
- I am open to new sources of wealth that the universe sends my way.
- My wealth is ever increasing.
- Things are always working out for me.
- All situations in my business are working for my good.
- I can increase my business bottom line to any number that I desire or choose.
- I have a healthy attitude toward money and am happy with getting more of it.
- I can advance as far in my career as I please.
- I can travel anywhere I want.
- I can learn any new skill I want to learn.

- I can become anything there is to become in this world.
- I am proud of others and happy for their success because I recognize that there is infinite wealth for everybody.
- The success of others doesn't come at my expense.
- We can all share in the universe's unlimited supply of wealth.
- My background, age, race, and gender do not limit my capacity to create unlimited wealth.
- There is an unlimited supply of customers who will pay me money for providing them value.
- The product, services, and skills I provide are worth paying for and will rightly make me rich.
- I approach learning with an enthusiasm which helps me grow to new heights.

- Every single day is an opportunity for new growth.
- I have all the abilities I need to grow rich and successful.
- I am intelligent and clever and there is no limit to how much more intelligent I can become.
- I believe in myself and my abilities to get things done.
- I always earn more money than I thought possible.
- My positive attitude draws money and abundance in my life.
- I create wealth through positive thoughts in my mind.
- I find it easy to meet my goals and this attracts more abundance.
- I continuously attract money and use it to do good for myself and for others.

- I give myself permission to be paid handsomely for the service I provide.
- I can have anything I want because the universe is good and generous.

I magnetically attract prosperity.

- My life is easier because I can draw on an infinite supply of wealth.
- Any company or project I create can become giant if I so choose.
- There is no skill I can't master.
- I choose to be wealthy and prosperous and to gain more wealth and prosperity every day.
- There is an endless supply of money and I can have as much as I want.
- An infinite amount of wealth already exists, and I am tapped into it.
- I can draw wealth from the infinite supply of the universe.

- Nobody can stop me from living up to my full potential.
- I will be the best at my chosen career.

Chapter 5

Money Mindset

Money is only a tool. It will take you wherever you wish, but it will not replace you as the driver." Who is credited with this famous quote?

The key to making money is to stay invested." Who expressed this insightful perspective?

The lack of money is the root of all evil." Who said this famous quote?

It's not about having money. It's about having power over money." Who is credited with this thought-provoking quote?

The more you learn, the more you earn." Who expressed this insightful perspective?

Money is like a sixth sense without which you cannot make a complete use of the other five." Who said this famous quote?

Wealth is the ability to fully experience life." Who expressed this profound perspective?

The only limit to our realization of tomorrow will be our doubts of today." Who is credited with this inspiring quote?

Money, like emotions, is something you must control to keep your life on the right track." Who said this famous quote?

The greatest wealth is to live content with little." Who expressed this meaningful perspective?

Answers

This quote is often attributed to American entrepreneur and author, Ayn Rand. She emphasizes that money is a tool that can help individuals achieve their goals and desires, but it is ultimately up to the individual to take control and make the necessary decisions to use money effectively.

This quote is commonly associated with American investor and philanthropist, Warren Buffett. He emphasizes the importance of long-term investing and staying committed to investment strategies rather than engaging in short-term trading or reacting to market fluctuations.

This quote is often attributed to American writer and humorist, Mark Twain. He plays on the common saying that "money is the root of all evil" by suggesting that it is actually the lack of money that can lead to undesirable consequences and unethical behavior.

This quote is commonly associated with American entrepreneur and author, Suze Orman. She emphasizes that true financial empowerment comes from having control and understanding of one's finances, rather than simply accumulating wealth without a purpose.

This quote is often attributed to American entrepreneur and motivational speaker, Warren G. Tracy. It highlights the correlation between continuous learning and financial success. By acquiring knowledge, skills, and expertise, individuals can enhance their earning potential and make more informed financial decisions.

This quote is often associated with British writer and philosopher, W. Somerset Maugham. He suggests that money is an essential tool that complements our other senses and abilities, enabling us to fully experience and navigate the world around us.

This quote is commonly attributed to American author and speaker, Henry David Thoreau. He believed that wealth should be measured not only in monetary terms but also by the richness of experiences and the ability to enjoy life to its fullest.

This quote is often associated with American president and entrepreneur, Franklin D. Roosevelt. He suggests that doubts and limiting beliefs can hinder our potential for financial success and personal growth. By embracing a positive mindset and believing in our abilities, we can overcome obstacles and realize our goals.

This quote is often attributed to American author and motivational speaker, Natasha Munson. It draws a parallel between managing money and managing emotions, highlighting the importance of maintaining control and balance to lead a fulfilling and prosperous life.

This quote is often attributed to ancient Greek philosopher, Plato. He believed that true wealth is not solely determined by material possessions but rather by finding contentment and satisfaction with what one already has.

Chapter 6

A Summary of Forgiveness, Awareness, and Unity

The Course of Magick contains many insights, ideas, and paths to obtain peace, love and forgiveness. One of the fundamental messages of the Course is the difference between reality and illusion and what is true about the way we think and what is false. For personal mastery, we must be able to identify what is part of our ego and what is part of our authentic self, or our spiritual self. The key to this first teaching is that nothing can really hurt what is inside of you, the real authentic you, your real spiritual self. Nothing can hurt that. No matter what happens to your physical body, there is a part of you that can never be hurt, which is part of the "Spirit of the

Universe" and part of God. To really come into a knowing-ness of this teaching, you must believe that you are connected to the source of creation and that you are a child of creation. Once you can deeply feel that connection between your spirit and the universe, then you are linked with that connection where you can finally reach your authentic power and your potential.

Now we realize that it may be difficult for many of you to believe in a power greater than yourself or a God of your understanding can be a challenge for some people, however, it must be said that if you can embrace the principles or the path, or you can embrace the spiritual philosophy and the love of the universe. The key, honestly, is acknowledging that you are not god, and you are not in total control. I understand that can be a hard thing to swallow for some, but when you let go and allow the universe to be your guide and to cooperate with The G-FORCE, you receive POWER. That means you are deliberately and intently and mutually operating with and in the universe. You find it is easier not playing god, and you understand that the universe is the greater force that you can cultivate for your advantage. As soon as you begin to cooperate with that force and that concept, then you can become harmonious with the creative power. To cultivate flow or be in tune with the spirit and unified with it, that is the Quantum Leap to obtain enthusiasm and empowerment. The second step is about reality and trying to attack it or protect yourself or separate from it. The ego is constantly talking to you, trying to protect your ego-self from other people, to make yourself feel better about yourself or sometimes it's trying to make you feel worse about yourself. The secret is to transcend that false ego and let go of that ego mind and self talk that is not real, it's just ego-chatter-based opinions. By letting go and learning to filter, you can connect with that spiritual self and your mind will no longer be a "house divided."

That real self is authentic and that real self knows that you ARE a good and whole and complete perfect being. Unfortunately for many of us, the ego is driven by pride, lust, anger, greed, gluttony, envy and sloth. Ego is even driven by subtle discouragement or justifiable resentment. So this false-mind and ego needs this ego-food to empower itself and the key for us to live happily and efficiently and effectively is to quit feeding the ego with this type of negative nutrition that it loves.

This separation between us as spiritual children from "A God of our understanding" is a fallacy in the clouded mind. The key to spiritual power is to clear away the wreckage of the past, to clear away the mental garbage, to dissipate the pride and the anger and the greed and the discouragement and the resentment, to let all of that go, push it aside, work through it, talk to other people about it, pray about it. Pray for those in our past, to let go of them. Do these things to receive this gift of cleansing and catharsis so we can reconnect to our Christ selves or our holy spirit.

Thus, the Magical Strategy IS the connection SECRET. Getting away from the separation and reconnecting to spiritual power is available for everyone who earnestly and sincerely wants it because it's always there. The miracle of unity is always available, the gift is always ready for those who are willing to accept it, but all of us must open our hearts and open our closed fists to receive this celestial reward.

Many hold on to old ideas and grievances. Many of us believe that we have sinned or that we have been bad people in the past, that we've done unforgivable harms. The real question of the day is will your God forgive you? Can you forgive yourself? And the answer is yes to both, if you are willing to allow yourself to be forgiven, if you are willing to forgive others and if you are willing to forgive God and if you are willing to allow God to forgive you. Then this forgiveness, this peace of mind, this peace that passeth all understanding can be available to you. It may take a little work but you can work through it. If you need help, you can always find a licensed counselor, a life coach, a priest, rabbi or an imam or even someone in a 12 step program. You can discuss privately these topics one-on-one and through private discourse. Also, you may discuss other important issues with your god of your personal understanding so that you may gain this peace and let go of these alleged sins. The objective is to put past ideas *which may be draining your energy* in the past because you need this purity of mind, this clarity of mind so you can stay connected and operate at a higher order of being.

There comes a point where all of us have an ego-voice that wants to blame others or use resentments to justify ourselves or justify the way we feel about other people. We were trying to blame people, places and things for the way we feel about ourselves, or we're trying to blame people and institutions for our failures. Or, we're trying to use our resentments, blame or anger to justify our guilt or to understand our shame. But there comes a point where each and every one of us needs to let go of our shame. There comes a point where all of us have to say, "Nobody can shame me anymore, nobody can shame the authentic spiritual self that you have inside you."

In many religions, there comes a point where you become reborn, reinvented, reconnected or even re-baptized as an adult and your faith becomes alive again. With faith and earnest beliefs, you transcend hope and knowingness. You can achieve this higher level of real belief and faith. Ultimately, if you can cultivate and develop faith, that is where real happiness and real peace of mind comes from, because you've altered your thought patterns to a higher dimension.

In spiritual programs, you might hear someone talk about a spiritual awakening, becoming awake spiritually or even developing a sixth sense or higher consciousness. In some of philosophies where people may NOT believe or recognize a god, there are countless seekers who have cultivated faith and belief in conjunction with a power greater than themselves which could be the principles, path, or other set of devout values.

To continue to grow spiritually, we need to work on what's called inner social justice or inner spiritual growth. Thus, if you are part of a spiritual program, it is contingent upon every one of us to build ourselves from the inside out using what is called "Inner Justice". Working on forgiveness, love, meditation, and love, we can continue to be in tune with the universe and solve our inner conflicts. This spiritual exercise allows us to maintain a harmonious relationship with ourselves, with God, with other people while improving self love, self regard, and love for the universe.

This is an extremely important magical and alchemical process, so let me say it one more time. The most important relationships you can cultivate is the one with yourself and your relationship with the force of the universe. By improving these mental concepts, you retrain your brain, create new empowering neuro-pathways, and the way you perceive yourself and your environment will dramatically improve.

The Holy Spirit.

What is that to us? Many people who have been reborn or reinvented in their faith because they have felt the spark of the inner Christ within them which may be called a reconnection. To put it into a simple allegory, let's pretend that there is a small fuse within your mind and that fuse can be blocked with emotions such as: anger and resentment or pride or jealousy or greed. All of these ills, what we would call deadly sins, affect the function of this "inner fuse of light".

Once you can clear out some of these blockages, like resentment, jealousy, anger or discouragement, the fuse lights up. And, that burning light is your connection between your spiritual self and the inner Christ which connects you to the source of all there is. This energy, enthusiasm, and the aliveness is the Holy Spirit, and that is what you hear people talk about who have been awakened.

It's a third force. It's you, the universe and something in-between that is a bright, magical connection and you know it when you have it. This inner awakening process does take persistence, but if you ask the universe to be connected to it, the power will materialize. If you ask for the release from bondage from self and from ego and ask for release from resentments and anger, blame, guilt and shame, then, you will know freedom. By doing all of these other things and allowing yourself to be set free, the inner-burning, bright, shining connection can be yours.

Some people in 12 step programs might call this bright light a "spiritual awakening" or some people might refer to this in A Course of Miracles as the "holy instant", a moment where your connection is realized and you know you are cooperating or participating with a power greater than yourself fueled by love and where the ego is not controlling you. Then we can heal our perception by individually forgiving the world. We can change our hearts and minds when we decide earnestly to expand the way we think by asking ask the universe for help and by praying to receive this gift of a superior perception. Then, we can become awakened and alive and aware for truly the first time.

Changing our minds about the world and allowing the Holy Spirit to heal the way we feel, to heal our worldview, to heal the way we think is ultimately the key to freedom. And, once you embrace this Holy Spirit or this spiritual awakening, then you will have this expanded perception.

But first, you need to remember that you must clear away the mental debris of the past create fresh, empty space within your heart and within your mind – for new LIFE , for new and good and wholesome beliefs. Once you have cleared away the old ideas and made room for some good, then the spirit of the universe lights up within you, this inner Christ and this inner connection to the Holy Spirit and the universe becomes alive. You, in turn, become energized and then the way you view the world at any given moment becomes clear and augmented. If you have a consciousness of wealth or a consciousness of happiness or a consciousness of peace, at any given moment, it will then color the way you perceive that moment and the way you give purpose and meaning to your life.

There are many ways to heal our perceptions, but one of the best methods is to renew the mind, forgive yourself, to forgive other people and to forgive God. We do this because, let's face it, there are two relationships that are most important in your life – the relationship with youself and the relationship with a power greater than yourself which most simply call GOD. These two relationships can make or break you. Those two relationships can make life easy or make life a struggle and as many spiritual programs profess, struggle is not necessary. Needless struggle is not mandatory. A lot of people, a lot of us, want to hold onto these old ways, hold onto these old habits, this old way of thinking because it gives us adrenaline and it makes us feel better than other people. It allows us to forget about our failures when, in fact, if we could let go of negative thinking and let go of these destructive habits, then our authentic selves can blossom and we can become who we really are meant to be. Further, we can become connected and have this intuition and this creativity that we're really supposed to utilize that makes us feel alive, that makes us feel authentic, and that makes us feel like we have purpose. Finally, we will then feel that we are truly heading down the path that we were always meant travel.

If you are having trouble with forgiveness, then we can offer several different methods to fix that problem or to cure that problem. The first one is every day when you wake up and every night before you go to bed, start saying affirmations aloud or to yourself or even in the mirror. You can write your own affirmations or you can go to the store and buy a book on affirmations and prayers to read silently or aloud. Many read these prayers or these meditations to themselves, or even read them out loud or to another person who loves and supports you.

Some may read them in conjunction with working with a spiritual counselor, sponsor, or a life coach. Read affirmative literature each day in the morning and in the evening and your beliefs and your worldview will change. Your vibration and energy will be altered upward. Your mindset will be enhanced and you will obtain a sense of excellence and poise.

Sometimes it takes 30 days before you even feel a major change or a major effect, but it will come quickly and powerfully. You may not even notice it but I promise you that if you do these practical-magical exercises for 30 days where you focus on gratitude, on peace of mind, & on forgiveness, you will become spiritually free and empowered.

If you have problems even beyond that, challenges even that you think are too heavy for basic prayers and affirmations, I recommend that you hit your knees every morning and every night and you ask directly to the God of your understanding for help. Or, you simply ask the Holy Spirit or Jesus Christ or ask your favorite Saint for intercession or assistance. It doesn't need to be perfect, as you simply need to humble yourself and tune in to the SOURCE and ask if you can be assisted and offer to cooperate. That's it. You will be amazed with the power you receive.

The key is that you earnestly make petition direct to God and say, "Please forgive me, please heal me, please remove my resentments, and please take away my dislike or my hatred for this person or for myself."

Or you may even pray for the happiness of another person or other individual, you pray earnestly and ask God to bless them and to take them away from your thinking. Ask your higher power to bless everyone, to bless those in your family, in your household, but most importantly, ask for grace for yourself, ask for peace for yourself, and ask for a thankful heart for yourself. Become a person who praises other people or even blesses your very self. Become a person who speaks of constructive and grateful and thankful things and if you do all of this, you will have what is called a grateful heart. You will have a firm belief and faith in the universe because it will change your faith in mankind. Many of us have had some really tough challenges. An example might be the death of someone close in your family or a family member or a great sickness or a catastrophic event such as a hurricane or a tsunami, whatever it might be. Some of us may have experienced a business divorce, a family divorce, your parents divorcing, or even yourself. All of these things can be extremely challenging and when we get into these situations that are extremely challenging, it's a call for many of us to rise to the occasion and become stronger.

Many times, we are going to have to release the other people that are involved whether it's a business problem with a partner or a lawsuit or a divorce or even a situation with our children. We're going to have to release people, release them with love, pray for them, pray that we can forgive them, and pray that they can forgive us. If we are able to do these things and to let go of what's hurting us and to become free and awake and aware while in forgiveness, all of these things provide us a true perception. This authentic perception looks past the bodily illusion to the light of Christ, and we will begin to see the little bit of God that is in all people.

When we finally reach this spiritual awake-ness and clarity, then the Holy Spirit will lift us up and make us whole. However, there is an investment that we have to make in maintaining this spiritual condition and a lot of it comes by using a basic methodology and some fundamental tools herein.

So to maintain our spiritual condition, we're probably going to need to do spiritual things and act responsibly. What we mean by that is to respond in a spiritual way to life and if that becomes difficult, of course, then you will have to continue to work the steps hitherto and continue to integrate the healthy virtues and ethics of the philosophy of your understanding or archetype.

We practice these spiritual exercises to maintain clarity, to maintain forgiveness, to maintain some sense of purity of mind. Purity of mind is where you are acting with love and unselfishness and you have a mindset of clear-and-convincing gratitude. That's what we mean by purity of mind and if you're doing things on a daily basis to maintain this quality of mind and quality of spirit and quality of perception, then that inner Christ, that inner light will remain bright and protect you because you will be acting in concert and in cooperation with the pure force of creation.

Similarly, many of us will need to deeply consider how we can continue to look at our character development. We enhance our character by observing the way we're acting, not acting, and the ways we're thinking. Maybe at the end of the day, take some notes about how you acted and think about ways that you can become a better person. Even 200+ years ago, Benjamin Franklin, in his autobiography, talked about his devotion to this evening practice of taking an inventory of his day with the motive of trying to become a better person tomorrow.

By prayer and meditation and maintaining this sufficient humility of which we've talked about, we will maintain some sense of clarity and spirituality in our lives. What we mean by humility are 4 key attributes: that you understand that you are teachable; that you understand your true authentic place in this world; that you are connected to a power greater than yourself; and that you understand who you really are. Humility is really the opposite of the insane ego-driven grandiosity or self-defeating thinking that inhibits our happiness. These practices are designed to eliminate the blocks to your connection to the spirit. If we desire to maintain our spiritual condition, then what will be important is our dedication to prayer, meditation, humility, clarity, love, and forgiveness. By virtue of our efforts, we become operative at a higher order and this higher state blesses us with a unity to a power greater than ourselves. Then, we finally understand our true identity and our sonship with God.

CHAPTER 7

The starting Point of All Achievement

Barnes' desire was not a hope or a wish; it was a burning, pulsing desire that outweighed everything else, and he succeeded because he chose a specific objective and focused all of his attention and effort on accomplishing it. It took sometime but he later achieved his desire.

Every human who understands the purpose of money wishes for it. Wishing will not bring riches but desiring riches with a state of mind that becomes an obsession , then planning definite ways and means to acquire riches, and backing those plans with persistence which does not recognize failure, will bring riches.

When you have a strong want to do anything, you will persuade yourself to do so by making a strategy, working toward it, and seizing every opportunity.

There is a distinction between desiring something and being prepared to get it. There are six practical procedures that can be used to convert a desire for wealth into its monetary counterpart.:

- Establish a definite date when you intend to possess the money you desire.
- Create a definite plan for carrying out your desire, and begin at once, whether you are ready or not, to put this plan into action.
- Write out a clear, concise statement of the amount of money you intend to acquire. Name the time limit for its acquisition. State what you intend to give in return for the

money, and describe clearly the plan through which you intend to accumulate it.
- Read your written statement aloud, twice daily, once just before retiring at night, and once after rising in the morning.
- Fix in your mind the exact amount of money you desire. Be definite as to the amount for there is a psychological reason for definiteness.
- Determine exactly what you intend to give in return for the money you desire. There is no such reality as 'something for nothing'.

You might think it's impossible to "imagine oneself in possession of money" before you actually do. This is where intense desire enters the picture. You will succeed in getting money if you sincerely want it with an obsession-level intensity. Having a strong desire for money and convincing yourself that you will succeed in getting it are the objectives.

All persons who have accumulated huge wealth have done a certain amount of dreaming, hoping, wishing, yearning, and planning before they became wealthy. As you plan your route to riches, don't let anyone convince you to write off the dreamer.

Go ahead and do what you want if it's the correct thing to do and you believe in it. Put your idea forward, and don't worry about what 'they' say if you fail, because 'they' may not realize that every failure contains the seed of an equal triumph.

Henry Ford, who was poor and illiterate, fantasized of a horseless vehicle. He got to work with whatever tools he had, rather than waiting for chance to favor him, and now the world is covered in evidence of his dream.

CHAPTER 8

THE PRINCIPLE OF POWER

When you become quiet, it just dawns on you

It is highly probable that you are reading these lines while browsing in one of the world's multitudinous bookstores, contemplating whether or not to part with your hard-earned money in order to purchase a book. After a cursory glance at the title chapters, what you read now will undoubtedly be the deciding factor in whether you make a purchase or place the book back on the shelf.

If I do have a claim to fame, it is generally recognized that I am a master of the Art of Persuasion. By using my art along with my knowledge of Dynamic Psychology it would be an extremely simple matter for me to contrive a convincing paragraph consisting of exactly what you want to hear; basically, how quickly and simply you can make your fortune and become an overnight success in whatever field you desire. Furthermore, I would convince you that we are both on the same wavelength and that I have a lot to say on a number of complex and controversial subjects that you will enjoy and appreciate. The proven method of inducing people to buy motivational books is to mix the basics up with a number of psychological words, a sprinkling of anecdotes, a liberal peppering of formulas, spread the mixture between the book covers with lashings of sincerity and persuasion and serve it up under the guise of a hypnotic "Get Rich Quick" title. Unfortunately, all too often, the readers of these books are the very same ones who complain quickly and bitterly that they have read reams of self-help material and still have not arrived at their goals.

This is the very bone of my contention. All too often self—help books are written with only one purpose in mind — to sell. The author himself may shy away from certain facts in fear of being labelled unorthodox, capitalistic, and even Machiavellian. Editors may reduce the copy still further by editing out certain facts they consider will not make good copy, and finally the publisher may insist on reducing the script even further by taking out something he considers too controversial. In this writing of each page to sell, instead of writing each page as it really is, the reader is often deprived of many of the facts he desperately needs in order to succeed. If you are one of the many who have read a lot of self-help material, but have always been left short or stranded high and dry, you can now appreciate why!

To say that I am not interested in selling this book would be stupid — of course I want it to sell. But more than that, I am genuinely interested in producing a book that is foolproof in its instructions on how to grow rich. I want to produce a book that will fill the needs of every person who has failed in his or her endeavors; in particular those people who have read a lot in order to attain their goals, but who still have not succeeded. For far too long the intelligence of the reading public has been insulted by having important questions answered with questions, or what amounts to a play on words. Certainly hundreds of times, if not thousands, we have been told, "It is all in the mind," or, similarly, "Everything begins with the mind." No one ever says, "If that is the case, why aren't all psychologists millionaires? Time and again we are informed that the average human being uses only 15 percent of his potential; never do we get a full explanation of why. Further- more we are never shown how to realize the remaining 85 percent.

Answering these questions formed the backbone of my research. Research, incidentally, that led me along many paths, up many blind alleys, and through much sifting of chaff from wheat. Ultimately, after many years of research my success philosophy is ready for the world. It will enable you to achieve your goals in the shortest possible time. It is a success philosophy to enable you to reach planes of abundance, have all the money you need to spend on your heart's desires and travel to all those exotic far off lands to see tranquil dawns and luminous dusks. It is your birthright to be able to obtain a pink Cadillac, a palatial Beverly Hills mansion complete with landscaped gardens, manicured lawns and a crystalline swimming pool and to be able to entertain frivolously, if that be your desire. Maybe you just want to get off the nine-to-five treadmill, or perhaps you have a very personal reason for wanting to be rich and famous. For all I know you are human like the rest of us and have funny quirks and traits. You may want riches to enable you to appear more attractive to the opposite sex. Perhaps you feel inferior and need wealth and recognition to show the world how great you are. It could be that you desire fame and fortune to compensate for some loss or misfortune. Whatever your reason, it is probably a good one!

Others will say some of life's finest things are not things. I agree, and there must be a way of achieving these intangible goals as well, whether they are peace of mind, love, health, happiness or power. One staggering fact presented itself early on in my research and gave a granite—like foundation to the success philosophy presented here. By observing the fact that Henry Ford never had an industrialist to inspire him to become the apostle of mass production, Andrew Carnegie never knew any tycoons to coax him into becoming a billionaire, and Edison did not have a scientist show him how to become the world's most celebrated inventor, I saw that none of these people had a success philosophy to follow, a sponsor to motivate them or a yardstick on which to gauge their success. Nor did they have self-help books to assist them. However, all of them excelled in their individual fields of endeavor. The Fords, Carnegies and Edison's of this world must have known some sort of secret or power to attain the phenomenal success each achieved in his particular vocation which, presumably, the layman had not heard of, nor had access to. I was particularly anxious to discover a common denominator, and whether that common denominator can still be applied to all human endeavors, even today. I found a common denominator of such extreme importance that it is outlined in detail in this very first chapter, entitled "The Principle of Power". Imagine wanting to become a doctor, scientist, toolmaker, airplane pilot, cordon bleu, or master of any worthwhile profession, art, craft, skill or vocation. Imagine wanting to become any of these by simply reading a book. It would be an absurd notion. Nobody would expect to master any of the above without long and thorough training, practice and study. However, when we enter the world of fame and fortune, the majority of contenders expect to achieve their goals merely by reading shortcut plans to riches — the doctor, scientist or toolmaker understands initially that he will work out a long apprenticeship, gradually gathering up knowledge from people already trained in his profession. He will take exams, learn, study and practice until he becomes proficient enough to work with his own skills, and eventually without the supervision of his superiors and instructors. The books he uses in his studies are tools. As from this very moment you become an apprentice. An Apprentice Millionaire, a Student of Success. No less!

The first thing the Apprentice Millionaire must do is learn to be patient. Before the brain surgeon can put a scalpel to flesh, make that first incision, he has a lot to learn about the brain. Before the Apprentice Millionaire can 'Talk and Grow Rich', he too has a lot to learn about the mind and brain. Not only his own — but also his prospects'. The starting point of my research was very simple. I wanted to find out if we really do use only 15 percent of our potential. If that were the case, I wanted to know how to tap the remaining 85 percent. I also wanted to know exactly what it is that is "all in the mind", and why "everything begins with the mind." I figured that if I knew the answers to these questions the acquiring of fame and fortune would be a relatively simple task. I took great pains to study much psychology and in doing so came across the brilliant works of the famous Swiss psychologist, Carl Jung. It was Jung's work that inspired me to do research along the particular lines that I chose. He, among others, noted that the people of the Eastern world are spiritually, mentally and physically more advanced than the people of the Western world. We in the Western world are materialistic, but the people of the Eastern world know how to train their minds to achieve incredible feats.

Through long and patient training of their subconscious minds, the mystics are able to perform unbelievable exploits. They train their minds to enable them to jab skewers in their backs and run needles through the palms of their hands without feeling pain or drawing blood. Although the Westerner has no use for the benefit of being able to perform such feats as these, we certainly do have a use for being able to control our minds so that we may prosper, and at the same time keep mentally and physically fit. All too often does the entrepreneur suffer from nervous exhaustion, stress, ulcers, lack of creative ideas and solutions to problems.

The obvious need (hence my research), was to harmoniously combine the knowledge of the East to complement the materialistic needs of the Westerner. One may call it turning Zen into Yen. The formula you need for all the wealth, success and achievement, and peace of mind, indeed for all the answers to all your problems, and I mean all, is $.$.$. SILENCE, STILLNESS AND SOLITUDE. This is no invention of my own, and research into psychology and studies of world leaders, scientists, musicians, physicists, industrialists, inventors and other famous people proves this great power has been used, unwittingly or intentionally, since the beginning of time. All human success and achievement stems from this one power. It was used by Mozart, Einstein, Carnegie, Shakespeare, Emerson and Edison, to mention a few. This is the power used by the fakirs and mystics of the East and the fire walkers of the Fiji Islands. This power enables the mystics to sit naked in the snow for long periods of time, lash their bodies with whips, drink poison, and to jab nails and skewers into their cheeks and backs without feeling pain or drawing blood. It allows the fire walkers to walk barefooted across red hot coals without feeling any pain. The secret lies in meditation, in Silence, Stillness and Solitude. We shall call this $.$.$.

You must take time out. You must empty your mind. It is no good trying to think of your problems and sort them out consciously. You have been doing that for years, and where has it got you? However hard you try consciously, it will never work out the way you want. The secret of meditation is to hand over your problems to the subconscious mind, which is the master mind, the largest mind, the powerful mind, the creative mind. Think of an iceberg. You know that only one-ninth of the iceberg is visible, and the other eight-ninths of it are below the surface. That huge mass below the surface can be likened to the powerful creative subconscious mind. The small portion on top, the one ninth, is likened to the conscious mind.

Unfortunately, it is the conscious mind we tend to use. Wrongly so, for it is non- creative. The powerful subconscious mind, however, will only operate if given periods of $.$.$. Alexander Graham Bell and Elmer Gates observed that the brain is both a receiving and a sending station for the vibration of thought. Imagine, then, sitting in a room with perhaps eight radios blaring away (for they, too, are receiving and sending stations) all of which are turned up to the same volume, but tuned into different frequencies. It would be impossible to decipher one from the other. For this same reason you can only hear your subconscious mind in $.$.$. Because, although you do not have eight radios blaring away, you do have a constant background of noise: telephones, radio, television; a motorcycle roars past, a child screams, a car revs up, a dog barks, an airplane flies over. The subconscious mind just cannot compete. Noise kills any hope of the subconscious mind communicating any enlightening ideas for the solving of problems, the making of money, the creating of happiness or the attainment of one's ambitions and goals. Noise kills genius! When the world's greatest inventor, Edison, was asked how he solved problems, he replied, "When you become quiet, it just dawns on you." You are not required to think. You must take time out to meditate. I say again, not to think — but to empty your mind. "Thinking is the most unhealthy thing in the world," wrote Oscar Wilde, "and people die of it just as they die of any other disease."

The first thing you must do is find a place of your own where nobody can disturb you. You must have silence, you must be still and you must be on your own. Forget the gum and cigarettes for just half an hour every day. After you have been practicing meditation for a number of weeks, you will find you like it so much, that it will become one or two hours instead of half an hour. Sit either on the floor or the bed, cross-legged, with your back reasonably straight and gently clasp your hands in front of you. This is a very basic Yoga lotus position. We can now assume you are in the desired position and have attained $.$.$. Now the secret is to empty your mind. This is more difficult than one would imagine. Try not to think of anything. Instead, concentrate on only one object. I choose to focus my attention on a glass prism, but any other object will do just as well. Just look at that object, think of nothing, breathe gently and relax. Try to think of absolutely nothing, for this is the secret of success.

To the layman this hardly seems a logical way of sorting out problems and generating "Success Ideas." It almost seems a waste of valuable time, with so much to do, so many pressures and problems. How then does it work? It is extremely simple. In the past you have let thoughts just fly through your mind, any thoughts at any time. Let us 'imagine that one hundred thoughts an hour go through your mind (in reality it is really thousands). If, in your meditation, you can reduce the number of thoughts going through your mind from one hundred an hour to only eighty thoughts an hour, that is an increase of 20 percent efficiency. If you can reduce the number of thoughts to only fifty an hour, that is an increase of 50 percent. The ultimate goal is to think of absolutely nothing. Then you can truthfully say that you have gained the power of concentrated thought by not thinking. It may seem paradoxical, but the mind is more creative when it is less active!

The great explorer, Rear Admiral Richard Byrd, understood what we are talking about. He was the Commanding Officer of the United States Antarctic Service Expeditions. On the eve of his departure from the Antarctic, he broadcast: "It was on my lonely vigil during the long Polar night that I learned the power of silence. The values and problems of life sorted out when I began to listen..." Adopt the attitude of listening; not thinking. Silence is golden, silence is gold! Because emptying your mind is so important, let us see. If we can make an extremely difficult task simpler. Make sure the place you choose for your meditation is someplace where you will not be disturbed. The thought of being disturbed will constantly go through your mind if you know that someone can barge in on you. Personally, I prefer to go right up into the hills, miles away from anywhere and anyone. This is not always practical, but it is absolutely necessary that no one be able to disturb you. Solitude is the nurse of wisdom. I know in some cities it is very difficult to achieve silence. Sometimes double glazing or storm windows reduce the noise level considerably. The local drugstore will supply you with wax ear plugs and the hardware store can usually supply earmuffs similar to those used by jackhammer operators.

I stress that noise kills genius. At first, you will find it difficult to sit still for half an hour, never mind a whole hour. You will probably get cramps and all sorts of uncomfortable feelings, but persevere; the rewards make it all worthwhile. Now for the actual emptying of your mind! The two things that will benefit your meditation greatly are a lighted candle and one of those digital clocks. To empty your mind for half an hour is not the easiest task in the world. However, until you become used to it, breaking down the half hour into thirty separate minutes is by far the easiest way of meditating. The idea is to say to yourself, "For the next minute I will think of nothing," stare blankly at the candle flame and think of nothing. Just wait for the next digit on the clock to come up. When it does, repeat the thought, that for another whole minute you will think of nothing. Just empty your mind and again wait for the next digit. You must bring to a halt the incessant chatter that goes on inside your skull, minute after minute, hour after hour, day after day, year in and year out. If you can turn down the noise in your mind, you can hear what else is going on. The noise machine in your brain box must be stopped!

It might help you to know I was a non-believer once, probably just as skeptical as you dashing here, there and everywhere at breakneck pace, one side of the country to the other, visiting my shops and my businesses everywhere, radio blaring away all the time. At that time I hadn't heard the German proverb that asks, "What is the use of running when we are not on the right road?" One of my companies collapsed. On top of that an employee embezzled a lot of money. Another company of mine was running at a loss. Thomas Fuller hit the nail on the head when he wrote, "He that is everywhere is nowhere." I was in such a state I could not think straight. I nearly burnt myself out. I thought I was going to self-destruct. I was numbed by it all, my brain nearly became addled. I found myself playing "Beat the Bailiff" and "Bounce the check." I didn't know which way to turn — until I discovered the $.$.$.

formula. I just started to sit still and empty my mind. Nothing at all happened for a number of weeks. Then things gradually started to take shape. I did not realize at the time I was unleashing a great power. Solutions to problems just came to me out of the blue. Illuminating ideas presented themselves and proved to be both practical and profitable, with unfathomable regularity. For once in my life things went right of their own accord; there was no help from me other than following through with the things my subconscious mind told me to do. I just sat still, quietly on my own, for an hour or two every day. Shakespeare wrote, "There's nothing so becomes a man as modest stillness," and Dr. Paul Brunton said, "I have found that stillness is strength."

CHAPTER 9

Principles of Think and Grow Rich: How to Use Your Mind to Create Wealth

Welcome to "The 7-Day Think and Grow Rich Challenge: Achieve Financial Success through Daily Actions" – a one-of-a-kind practical workbook that will ignite the flames of ambition within you and guide you towards the path of abundance and prosperity. This book, my little gem of wisdom, will serve as your compass, your guardian angel, your trusted companion on this extraordinary journey towards financial liberation.

Now, before we dive headfirst into this captivating venture, let me take a moment to introduce myself. My name is Saratha Ravichandran, and my journey towards financial success has been nothing short of a magical odyssey. Born into a humble family, we knew the meaning of sacrifice and hard work all too well. But like a shooting star streaking across the night sky, I was determined to rise above my circumstances and create a life of abundance.

It was during my college years that I stumbled upon the magnificent teachings of personal finance and investing. Pages flew beneath my fingertips as I eagerly devoured every word, gleaning the secrets that held the key to my future success. The 13 principles of Think and Grow Rich captivated me, like a spellbinding melody that resonated deep within my soul. And so, armed with this newfound knowledge and an unwavering determination, I set forth on my path to greatness.

As the years unfolded, I crafted my destiny, brick by brick, day by day. I laid the foundation of my dreams, nurturing them with unwavering faith and determination. It wasn't always easy, my dear reader. Oh no, far from it. There were times when doubt clawed at my resolve, threatening to crumble the walls I had so meticulously built. But like a phoenix rising from the ashes, I emerged stronger, more determined than ever before.

And so, here I stand, a beacon of hope amidst a sea of uncertainty, ready to share with you the incredible wisdom that has transformed my life. "The 21-Day Think and Grow Rich Challenge" is my humble gift to you — a roadmap, if you will, leading you towards the treasure trove of abundance that lies within your grasp.

Within these pages, we will embark on a remarkable journey of self-discovery and transformation. Each day, we will unravel the mysteries of financial success through practical exercises and thought-provoking reflections. In this enchanted labyrinth of dreams and aspirations, you will cultivate the mindset of a champion, honing your skills, acquiring knowledge, and embracing the power that lies within.

From the very first day, you will unleash the power of your desires, infusing them with an intensity that will ignite a fire within your soul. You will ponder upon the evidence of your own capabilities, gazing into the mirror of self-belief with unwavering confidence. Affirmations will roll off your tongue, like a sacred chant, empowering you with each whispered word.

But we shall not stop there, my dear reader, for we shall forge ahead towards the future you envision. Step by step, we shall craft a plan of action, a roadmap to success that will guide you towards your goal. Challenges may arise, my dear reader, but you hold within you the power to overcome them. Fueled by an unwavering determination, you shall emerge victorious, a warrior brimming with triumph.

Just as the river meanders through the lush valleys, so too shall we explore the realms of intuition, tapping into the wellspring of wisdom that lies within. We shall stretch the limits of our minds, embracing knowledge and challenges with open arms. And as we seize the present, we shall be intoxicated by the breath of the future, dancing upon the winds of possibility.

Through thick and thin, we shall band together, a circle of support and camaraderie. For in this world of dreams and aspirations, surrounding ourselves with like-minded souls is the secret ingredient to our success. Together, we shall celebrate our victories, both big and small, rejoicing in the tapestry of accomplishments woven from our collective efforts.

As we draw near to the grand finale, we shall remember the importance of resilience and perseverance. Like a mighty oak tree, we shall stand tall amidst the storms of life, unyielding in the face of adversity. And never, oh never, shall we forget to revel in the magical tapestry of gratitude, for it is through this kaleidoscope of appreciation that our souls shall be replenished.

Let's see the Key Principles of "Think and Grow Rich" and The Golden Rule:

- The Sex Transmutation: You can transmute your sexual energy into creative energy to achieve your goals.

- The Subconscious Mind: You can use your subconscious mind to achieve your goals by programming it with autosuggestion.
- The Brain: You can use your brain to create new ideas and solve problems.
- The Sixth Sense: You can develop your sixth sense to receive guidance and insights from the universe.
- The Golden Rule: Treat others with kindness and respect, and you will create a positive ripple effect that will come back to you in the form of financial success.
- Desire: The starting point of all achievement is desire. You must have a burning desire to achieve your financial goals in order to succeed.
- Faith: You must have faith in yourself and your ability to achieve your goals.

- Autosuggestion: You can use autosuggestion to program your subconscious mind for success.
- Specialized Knowledge: You must have specialized knowledge in the field in which you want to achieve success.
- Imagination: You must use your imagination to create a blueprint for your success.
- Organized Planning: Once you have a blueprint for your success, you must create a plan to achieve it.
- Decision: You must be decisive and take action towards your goals.
- Persistence: You must be persistent in your efforts, even when faced with setbacks.
- The Mastermind Alliance: You can accelerate your success by forming a mastermind alliance with other successful people.

The science behind the 7-day challenge

The 21-Day Think and Grow Rich Challenge is a self-improvement challenge that is designed to help you achieve your financial goals. The challenge is based on the 13 principles of Think and Grow Rich, a book by Napoleon Hill that is considered to be one of the most influential personal development books of all time.

The challenge is simple: for 21 days, you will focus on one of the 13 principles of Think and Grow Rich and complete a daily exercise related to that principle. By the end of the challenge, you will have a deeper understanding of the principles of Think and Grow Rich and how to apply them to your life.

Why 7 Days?

There is a scientific basis for the 7-day challenge. According to research, it takes an average of 7-days to form a new habit. This means that if you consistently practice a new behavior for 21 days, it is more likely to become a habit.

The 7- Day Think and Grow Rich Challenge is designed to help you form new habits that will lead to financial success. By focusing on one principle at a time and completing a daily exercise, you will be able to internalize the principles and make them part of your everyday routine.

In the 7- Day Think and Grow Rich Challenge, you embark on a journey of habit transformation. Whether it's adopting a new habit or refining an existing one, you commit to 7- days of practice, improvement, and unwavering consistency.

Day-1: Desire Unveiled: Igniting the Spark of Achievement

Thought for the day: Clarity about your desires is the first spark needed to ignite the fire of achievement.

I knew that it was essential to start by identifying and clarifying my deepest desires and ambitions. I understood that without a clear vision of what I wanted to achieve, it would be difficult to create a roadmap towards financial success.

I found a quiet corner in my home, away from distractions, and sat down with a pen and a notebook. Closing my eyes, I took a deep breath and allowed my mind to wander freely. I delved into the depths of my soul, searching for the aspirations that had been hidden beneath the surface for far too long.

In that moment of reflection, I realized that my ultimate desire was to achieve not just financial success, but also a sense of fulfilment in all aspects of my life. I wanted to create a legacy that would make a positive impact on the world, while also enjoying the freedom and security that financial abundance can provide.

I grabbed my pen and began to write, capturing my desires in clear and specific terms. I envisioned a life where I could travel the world, immerse myself in new cultures, and make a difference in the lives of others. I wanted to build a successful business that would not only provide for my own needs, but also create opportunities for others to thrive.

As the words flowed onto the pages of my notebook, I felt a surge of excitement and determination. Each sentence became a declaration of my commitment to achieving these desires. I knew that by putting them into writing, I was setting the stage for the manifestation of my dreams.

Having completed the task, I took a moment to ponder the thought provided for the day. The words echoed in my mind, "Clarity about your desires is the first spark needed to ignite the fire of achievement." I realized the wisdom in those words, for how could I expect to attain something if I was not even clear about what it was that I truly wanted?

With newfound clarity and a written representation of my desires, I felt a renewed sense of purpose and direction. I knew that the next steps in this challenge would require taking action, but I also understood that this first day had laid the foundation for everything that would follow.

I closed my notebook, a smile of anticipation curving my lips. I was ready to embark on this journey towards financial success, armed with a clear vision of what I wanted to achieve and a deep understanding that it all started with the simple act of reflection.

Action Steps for Day 1:

1.
2. **Set Aside Quiet Time: Allocate a dedicated and distraction-free space and time for reflection. Find a peaceful corner in your environment where you can sit comfortably and concentrate.**
3. **Deep Breathing Exercise: Begin your session with a few deep breaths to relax your mind and body. Close your eyes if**

it helps you focus and calm your thoughts.
4. **Identify Your Deepest Desires:** Take this time to delve into your inner self and uncover your most profound desires and ambitions. What do you truly want to achieve in your life?
5. **Write Them Down:** With a pen and notebook or a digital note-taking tool, start writing down your desires in clear and specific terms. Be as detailed as possible, describing what success looks like to you.
6. **Visualize Your Desires:** As you write, imagine yourself living the life you desire, experiencing the fulfilment of your aspirations. This visualization can help reinforce your commitment.

7. **Set Your Goals: Transform your desires into actionable goals. Define specific steps and milestones that will lead you toward achieving these desires.**

Day-2 : Burning Desire: The Driving Force to Achieve Goals

Thought for the day: An intense, emotionally charged desire becomes the driving force behind your actions and decisions. It propels you towards your goals.

As I sat down with pen and paper, ready to revisit my written desire from yesterday, I could feel the anticipation building inside me. This task held the potential to further ignite the fire within, to give it that extra boost of intensity and emotion, which would propel me closer to my goals.

I closed my eyes, taking a deep breath to centre myself, and then opened them to the empty page before me. I began by reading the desire I had written yesterday, the words that had started to shape my dreams, my vision of the life I wanted to create.

But now, it was time to go deeper. It was time to paint a vivid picture of what achieving this desire would look like, feel like, and sound like. I wanted to create a scene so real in my mind, a scene that would fuel me with even more determination and drive.

I imagined myself standing on a stage, facing a crowd of eager listeners. I could feel the warmth of the spotlight on my face, illuminating my every feature. The air crackled with anticipation as I took a moment to soak in the energy of the room.

In this moment, I imagined the benefits and positive impact that achieving my desire would have on my life. Financial success would bring me the freedom to live life on my own terms, to explore the world and experience new adventures. It would mean the ability to provide for my loved ones, to give back to those less fortunate, and to make a lasting difference in the lives of others.

I envisioned the smile on my parents' faces, the pride they would feel knowing that their sacrifices had not been in vain. The thought of being able to support them in their retirement years brought tears to my eyes. It would be a fulfilment of their dreams as much as mine.

I imagined the impact it would have on my own confidence and self-belief. The knowledge that I had set a goal, worked tirelessly towards it, and finally achieved it would be a constant reminder of my own capabilities. It would fuel the fire within to tackle even greater challenges and reach even greater heights.

As I allowed myself to fully immerse in this vision, the emotions came flooding in. Gratitude for the opportunities that lay ahead, excitement for the journey that awaited me, and determination to make this vision a reality. This intense, emotionally charged desire was now firmly planted in my heart and mind, ready to drive me forward.

I knew that this desire would become the guiding force behind all my actions and decisions. It would be the fuel that propelled me towards my goals, even when the path ahead seemed arduous. With this unwavering desire burning within me, I could face any obstacle, overcome any setback, and emerge stronger than ever.

I closed my eyes and held on to this feeling, capturing every ounce of intensity and emotion within me. I allowed it to seep into my very being, fuelling my determination and fortifying my resolve.

With this renewed sense of purpose, I picked up my pen and began to add these vivid details and emotional charge to my written desire. I knew that every word, every thought, and every feeling would further solidify this desire in my heart, and bring me one step closer to achieving the financial success I so deeply craved.

And as I wrote, the words flowed effortlessly, as if guided by a force greater than myself. I knew then, that this intense, emotionally charged desire had become my driving force, my beacon of light in the pursuit of my dreams.

Action Steps for Day 2:

- Review Your Written Desire: Begin by revisiting the desire you wrote down previously. Take a moment to read and reflect on it, reminding yourself of what you want to achieve.

- Boost Self-Confidence: Recognize how achieving this desire will boost your self-confidence and self-belief. Embrace the knowledge that you are capable of setting and accomplishing significant goals.
- Embrace Intensity and Emotion: Allow intense emotions to flood your visualization. Feel the desire burning within you, driving you forward with unwavering determination.
- Capture the Experience in Writing: Open your eyes and pick up your pen or keyboard. Begin to describe the vivid mental scene and emotions you experienced during your visualization. Write down every detail, making it as vivid as possible.
- Affirm Your Commitment: As you write, affirm your commitment to pursuing this desire with

unwavering determination. Declare that this intense, emotionally charged desire will guide your actions and decisions.

- Create a Vivid Mental Scene: Close your eyes, take a deep breath, and imagine a detailed, emotionally charged scene related to your desire. Picture yourself in that scenario as if it's happening right now.
- Engage All Senses: As you visualize, involve all your senses. Notice what you see, hear, feel, smell, and even taste in this scenario. Make it as real and immersive as possible.
- Focus on the Benefits: While in this mental scene, emphasize the positive impact and benefits achieving your desire will bring to your life. Feel the emotions associated with these benefits, such as joy, pride, and gratitude.

- Connect with Loved Ones: Envision how your success will positively affect your loved ones, whether it's providing for them, supporting their dreams, or making them proud. Feel the emotions tied to these connections.

These exercises will help you to Clarify your desire and make it more specific. When you can vividly imagine what achieving your desire would look like, feel like, and sound like, it becomes more real to you and easier to stay focused on. It Increases your emotional attachment to your desire. The more emotionally charged your desire is, the more motivated you will be to take action towards achieving it. It creates a driving force for your actions and decisions. When you have a clear and compelling vision of what you want to achieve, it will guide your every move and help you to make choices that are aligned with your goals.

Day-3 : Faith Renewed: The Strength of Past Success

Thought for the day: Remembering past successes reinforces your self-belief and demonstrates the power of faith.

As I sit down to complete the task for Day 3 of the 21-Day Think and Grow Rich challenge, I find myself transported back in time to those moments in my life when I believed in myself and achieved something truly noteworthy. These instances are not just mere memories; they are the pillars upon which I have built my self-belief and confidence.

The first moment that comes to mind took place during my college years. I was studying for a major exam and had invested countless hours in preparing for it. Doubt and anxiety crept into my mind as I questioned my abilities. But deep down,

I knew that I had put in the effort and possessed the knowledge necessary to succeed. Pushing those negative thoughts aside, I embraced a positive mindset and entered the exam room with determination. When the results were announced, I had scored the highest in the class. It was a pivotal moment that reminded me of the immense power of believing in oneself.

Another significant instance occurred when I launched my own business. As a young entrepreneur with limited resources, the odds seemed stacked against me. However, I refused to let the fear of failure hold me back. I believed in my idea, my drive, and my ability to innovate. I poured my heart and soul into building my business from the ground up, facing countless challenges along the way. Yet, with unwavering self-belief, I pushed forward. The moment of triumph came when I secured a crucial partnership with a major company, a deal that would propel my business into success. It was a testament to the power of faith and the rewards that come with unwavering determination.

Reflecting on these past successes brings a renewed sense of self-belief surging through my veins. It serves as a reminder that I am capable of achieving greatness, no matter the obstacles that lie in my path. Each achievement is like a milestone on a journey towards success, reminding me of the strength and resilience that resides within me.

Writing down these instances not only helps me in this 21-Day challenge but also serves as a repository of inspiration. It is a personal record of my triumphs and a reminder of the power that lies within my own mind. As I read through these achievements, I am filled with a sense of gratitude and appreciation for the journey that I have undertaken.

Moving forward, I will strive to recall these moments of self-belief and accomplishment throughout my daily life. They will serve as a beacon of light during moments of doubt and uncertainty, reminding me of the greatness that resides within me. By harnessing the power of faith and self-belief, I am confident that I can continue to achieve remarkable things and fulfill my financial aspirations.

With this task completed, I am eager to move forward in this 21-Day challenge, armed with the memories of my past successes and a renewed sense of self-belief. I am ready to embrace the power of faith and take the necessary daily actions to achieve financial success. The journey continues, and I am excited to see where it will lead me.

Action Steps for Day 3:

- Reinforce Self-Belief: As you write, reflect on how these past successes reinforced your self-belief. Recognize the power of faith and determination that played a role in your achievements.
- Create a Repository of Inspiration: Consider compiling these written success stories into a personal document or journal. This will serve as a repository of inspiration that you can revisit whenever you need a boost of self-belief.
- Set Reminders: Make it a habit to revisit these stories regularly, especially during moments of doubt or uncertainty. Use them as

reminders of your capabilities and past triumphs.
- Apply Lessons to Current Goals: Identify how the lessons learned from these past successes can be applied to your current financial aspirations and other goals.
- Practice Gratitude: Express gratitude for these past achievements and the lessons they've taught you. Gratitude can further reinforce your positive mindset.
- Take Daily Actions: Commit to taking daily actions aligned with your financial goals, fueled by the belief in your abilities and the power of faith. Use your past successes as motivation to keep moving forward.
- Reflect on Past Successes: Set aside some time to recall significant moments in your life when you believed in yourself and achieved notable success. These moments should

demonstrate your ability to overcome challenges and obstacles.
- Identify Key Successes: Choose at least two of these moments that stand out the most to you. These could be academic achievements, personal milestones, career successes, or any other significant accomplishments.
- Analyse Your Mindset: For each chosen success, analyse your mindset leading up to and during that achievement. What positive beliefs or attitudes did you hold? How did you overcome doubt or fear?
- Write Them Down: Document these moments of success and the associated mindset on paper or digitally. Be detailed and specific about each experience.

Day-4: Action Fuels Faith: Steps Toward Great Achievements

Thought for the day: Faith is strengthened through action. As you take small steps, your self-belief grows, paving the way for larger achievements.

As I sat down to tackle Day 4 of the Think and Grow Rich Challenge, I pondered over the task at hand. Identifying a small, achievable goal that aligned with my larger aspirations seemed like a daunting task. How could I possibly choose just one goal from the myriad possibilities that lay before me? Nonetheless, I knew that in order to make progress on my journey to financial success, I had to start somewhere.

I closed my eyes and took a deep breath, allowing my mind to quieten and focus. I reflected on my ultimate aspirations, the dreams that motivated me to embark on this challenge. I pictured myself achieving financial freedom, living a life filled with abundance and success. It felt exhilarating, and yet, somewhat distant. I needed a stepping stone, a tangible objective that would serve as a building block towards my grand vision.

And then it hit me. I had always dreamt of starting my own online business selling handmade jewelry, a project that combined my passion for creativity and entrepreneurship. It was a goal that held personal significance to me, and I believed that by taking action in this realm, I could not only prove to myself the validity of the Think and Grow Rich principles but also take a concrete step in the direction of my broader aspirations.

Excitement surged through my veins as I opened my laptop and began researching the steps required to start an online jewelry business. I familiarized myself with the market, explored potential suppliers, and studied successful entrepreneurs in the industry. With a notebook by my side, I jotted down ideas, sketched out designs, and brainstormed strategies for branding and marketing.

Although these initial actions may have seemed small in the grand scheme of things, they were instrumental in kindling my faith, my unwavering belief in my ability to achieve success. Each deliberate step I took towards launching my online jewelry business further solidified my conviction in the Think and Grow Rich principles. I realized that faith alone was not enough; it needed to be accompanied by action.

Through this experience, I learned that faith is a catalyst for progress, but it is through action that faith becomes strengthened. Every small step I took, no matter how seemingly insignificant, served to build my self-belief and propel me forward. I found solace in the fact that my daily actions were like seeds, planted in the fertile soil of my unwavering faith, ready to bear fruit in the form of future achievements.

As I continued my journey through the Think and Grow Rich Challenge, I carried the lesson of Day 4 with me. I understood the power of taking small, concrete actions towards my goals, and the impact it could have on my overall success. With each passing day, my self-belief grew stronger, my faith rejuvenated, and my determination amplified.

I was ready to face the challenges that lay ahead, armed with the unwavering belief that as I continued to take small steps towards my larger aspirations, my faith would be justified, and my dreams would become my reality.

Action Steps for Day 4:

- Research and Plan: Begin researching and planning the necessary steps to achieve this small goal. If it's related to a business venture, like the example of starting an online jewelry business, investigate the market, suppliers, and strategies.
- Set Deadline: Set deadlines for each step and track your progress.
- Take Action: Take action towards your goal on a daily basis, no matter how small.
- Reflect on Your Ultimate Aspirations: Take some time to contemplate your long-term goals and ultimate aspirations, particularly in the context of your financial success.
- Choose a Tangible, Small Goal: Identify a small, achievable goal that aligns with your larger financial aspirations. Make sure your

goal is specific, measurable, achievable, relevant, and time-bound.
- Write Down Your Chosen Goal: Write down your goal in clear and specific terms.
- Break it into Smaller Steps: Break down your goal into smaller, more manageable steps.

Goal:

Steps:

- Record and edit the course videos.
- Create a landing page and launch the course.
- Research the market and identify a target audience.
- Develop a course outline and create a content plan.

Deadlines:

- Research the market: 1 week
- Develop course outline: 2 weeks

- Create content plan: 2 weeks
- Record and edit course videos: 4 weeks
- Create landing page and launch course: 2 weeks

Once you have set a goal and broken it down into steps, you can start taking action towards your goal on a daily basis. Even small steps, such as researching the market or developing a course outline, can make a big difference over time.

As you take action towards your goal, your faith in your ability to succeed will grow stronger. Remember, faith is strengthened through action. So keep taking small steps, and eventually, you will reach your goal.

Day-5: Affirmation Alchemy: Shaping Your Financial Destiny

Thought for the day: Positive affirmations are the keys to unlocking your true potential. They bridge the gap between desire and belief, paving the way for success.

To begin, I take a few moments to reflect on my deepest desires and goals. I ask myself what I truly want to achieve in terms of financial success. Once I have a clear picture in my mind, I start crafting positive affirmations that align with my desires.

I write each affirmation in the present tense, as if it is already true. For example, if my desire is to earn a six-figure income, I might create an affirmation such as, "I am a successful six-figure earner." I repeat this affirmation to myself, allowing the words to sink deeply into my subconscious mind.

But reciting affirmations is just the beginning. To enhance the effectiveness of this practice, I decided to make a recording of myself repeating these affirmations. I find a quiet space where I won't be disturbed, and I speak my affirmations into a recording device, making sure to infuse each word with confidence and belief.

After creating the recording, I save it on my phone and commit to listening to it every day. Whether it's during my morning routine, while commuting to work, or before bed, I find a quiet moment to play the recording and absorb the positive messages it contains. Each time I listen to my affirmations, I can feel the energy and determination building within me.

But affirmations alone are not enough. I understand that the environment in which I surround myself plays a crucial role in shaping my mindset and beliefs. So, I take the opportunity to assess my surroundings and make intentional changes to create a positive and uplifting atmosphere.

I adorn my workspace and living areas with images and messages that inspire and motivate me. I print out pictures of my dream house, luxury cars, or dream vacation destinations and hang them where I can see them every day. Seeing these visuals reminds me of my goals and keeps my desire alive.

In addition to images, I also surround myself with positive messages. I write uplifting quotes and encouraging statements on sticky notes and place them strategically around my home and office. Every time my eyes land on these messages, I am reminded of my potential and the power I have within me to achieve my desires.

As day 5 of the challenge comes to a close, I reflect on the power of positive affirmations and the impact of creating an environment filled with positivity. I am committed to repeating my affirmations daily and immersing myself in an atmosphere that uplifts and motivates me.

Tomorrow, I will dive deeper into the power of visualization and the role it plays in manifesting my desires. But for now, I rest, knowing that every positive affirmation and every image surrounding me is guiding me closer to the financial success I seek.

Action Steps for Day 5:

- Listen to Your Recording Daily: Commit to listening to your recorded affirmations every day. Incorporate this practice into your daily routine, whether it's in the morning, during your commute, or before bedtime.

- Enhance Your Environment: Assess your surroundings and make intentional changes to create a positive and uplifting atmosphere.
- Display Positive Messages: Surround yourself with images and messages that inspire and motivate you. Place them strategically around your home and workplace where you'll frequently see them. These messages should inspire and remind you of your potential.
- Clarify Your Desires: Identify your deepest desires and goals related to financial success.
- Craft Positive Affirmations: Write positive affirmations in the present tense, as if your desires are already true. Be specific in your affirmations. The more specific you are, the more powerful your affirmations will be. Use strong and positive language. Avoid using

negative words or phrases in your affirmations.

- Record Your Affirmations: Take the time to record your affirmations. Use your phone or any other device to capture yourself repeating them.
- Repeat or Listen to your affirmations regularly, especially when you are feeling discouraged or unmotivated. Be patient and persistent. It takes time and effort to reprogram your subconscious mind. By following these steps, you can harness the power of positive affirmations and create an environment that supports your financial success journey.

Day-6: The Learning Mindset: Unlocking Your Potential for Financial Success

Thought for the day: Learning is the compass that guides you towards your financial goals, illuminating the path to success.

For me, one of the crucial skills I needed to acquire was marketing. In order to grow my business and reach a wider audience, I knew I needed to understand the intricacies of marketing and branding. So, I began my research journey, eager to find the best resources and courses to help me acquire this knowledge.

I started by immersing myself in books and online articles written by marketing experts. These comprehensive guides provided a solid foundation and introduced me to the different marketing strategies and techniques that were available. However, I also recognized that simply reading about marketing wasn't enough. I needed a more hands-on approach to truly understand and apply these concepts.

That's when I came across an online course offered by a renowned marketing professional. The course promised to provide practical exercises and real-world examples to help students grasp the nuances of marketing. It was exactly what I was looking for. Without hesitation, I enrolled in the course, ready to gain the skills necessary to take my business to new heights.

In addition to the online course, I also sought out networking opportunities with other professionals in the marketing field. Attending industry conferences and joining relevant associations allowed me to tap into a wealth of knowledge and connect with people who shared my passion for marketing.

As I immersed myself in this world of lifelong learning, I realized that acquiring new skills and expanding my knowledge was not only beneficial for my business but also for my personal growth. Lifelong learning became a mindset, a way of life that allowed me to continuously evolve and adapt to new challenges.

Throughout this journey, I discovered that there were countless resources and courses available to acquire the knowledge I needed. The key was to remain open-minded and proactive in seeking out these opportunities. Whether it was online tutorials, workshops, or mentorship programs, I made a commitment to always be on the lookout for ways to expand my skill set.

Day 6 of the 21-Day Think and Grow Rich Challenge reminded me of the power of lifelong learning. By identifying the skills and knowledge crucial to my goals and actively seeking out resources and courses, I was investing in my future success. I embraced the idea that learning is a continuous process and that, as long as I maintained a growth mindset, there would always be opportunities to further develop myself.

So, my advice to you on Day 6 is simple – identify the areas in which you need to grow and develop, and then research available resources and courses to acquire the knowledge you need. Be proactive and embrace lifelong learning as a crucial component of your journey to financial success. Remember, the more you learn, the more you can achieve.

Action Steps for Day 6:

- Network: Connect with other professionals in your field. Attend industry events and join relevant associations to network with people who can share their knowledge and expertise with you.

- Set a Learning Schedule: Set aside time each week for learning. Even if it's just for an hour, make a commitment to dedicate some time to reading, taking courses, or learning something new.
- Track Your Progress: Keep a record of the skills and knowledge you've acquired along your learning journey. Regularly assess your progress and adjust your learning plan as needed.
- Identify: Make a list of your financial goals. Once you have a clear understanding of your goals, you can start to identify the skills and knowledge you need to achieve them.
- Research: Research online courses, workshops, and mentorship programs. There are many different resources available to help

you learn new skills and expand your knowledge.

Here is an example of a specific action you could take on Day 6:

- Find an online course on a skill that is essential for your financial goals. For example, if you want to start your own business, you could find a course on marketing, accounting, or business law.
- Enroll in the course and commit to completing it within a set timeframe.
- Set aside time each week to work on the course and learn the new skills.
- Apply the skills you learn to your work or business.
- By taking this specific action, you can start to develop the skills and knowledge you need to achieve your financial goals.

By following these steps, you can make lifelong learning a part of your journey to financial success. Remember, the more you learn, the more you can achieve.

Day-7: The Path to Knowledge: Crafting Your Learning Plan for Success

Thought for the day: The path to knowledge is not a solo journey; it is a continuous exploration. The more we open our minds to learning, the more opportunities we create for growth and success. By crafting this plan, I am taking deliberate steps towards realizing my dreams. I am committed to acquiring the necessary skills and knowledge to achieve financial success.

As I sat down with my notebook and pen, I couldn't help but feel a surge of excitement. This was the moment where I would take concrete steps towards transforming my life. I knew that crafting a well-thought-out learning plan would be crucial in maximizing the benefits of the resource I had chosen.

First, I decided to set aside dedicated time each day for my learning journey. I knew that consistency and discipline were key, so I scheduled two hours every morning before starting my workday. This would ensure that I had ample time to delve deep into the material, without any interruptions or distractions.

Next, I broke down the resource into smaller sections, allowing myself to gradually absorb the information without feeling overwhelmed. I made a detailed outline of each chapter or module, highlighting key points and concepts that I wanted to focus on. This approach would not only help me retain the information better but also provide a clear roadmap of my progress.

To keep myself engaged and motivated, I decided to incorporate various learning methods. Alongside reading the resource, I planned to listen to podcasts or watch educational videos related to the topic. This way, I would be able to reinforce my understanding through different mediums and gain additional perspectives.

Understanding the importance of reflection and application, I also dedicated time each day **to** journaling. I would write down my thoughts and insights from the material, as well as any ideas or action steps that emerged. This practice would not only help me internalize the knowledge but also serve as a valuable resource for future reference.

As I finished outlining my learning plan, a thought crossed my mind:

The path to knowledge is not a solo journey; it is a continuous exploration. The more we open our minds to learning, the more opportunities we create for growth and success. By crafting this plan, I am taking deliberate steps towards realizing my dreams. I am committed to acquiring the necessary skills and knowledge to achieve financial success."

With these words echoing in my mind, I closed my notebook and felt an immense sense of pride and purpose. I knew that this learning plan would be the backbone of my transformation, guiding me through the remaining days of this challenge and beyond. I was ready to embark on this journey, armed with a clear roadmap towards the future I desired.

Action Steps for Day 7:

- Mastering Concepts: Break down the resource into smaller sections.
- Active Learning: Make a detailed outline of each section, highlighting key points and concepts.
- Incorporate Multiple Learning Methods: Incorporate various learning methods, such as reading, listening to podcasts, and watching educational videos.
- Study journaling: Dedicate time each day to journaling your thoughts, insights, ideas, and action steps.
- Learning Plan: Craft a learning plan for the resource you have chosen.
- Set Dedicated Learning Time: Set aside dedicated time each day for your learning

journey. Schedule time each day for your learning, even if it's just for 30 minutes.
- Distraction Free Space: Create a dedicated space for learning, free from distractions.

By following these actionable tasks, you'll create a structured and effective learning plan that will guide you on your journey to acquiring the necessary skills and knowledge for financial success. Your commitment to continuous exploration and growth will be a driving force in achieving your goals.

www.ingramcontent.com/pod-product-compliance
Lightning Source LLC
LaVergne TN
LVHW010217070526
838199LV00062B/4639